LILIAN DAYTON

PUBLISHING IMPRINT

The Ultimate Guide on How to Publish Faster to Make More Profit, Learn Effective Strategies on How to Come up and Publish Content Faster

Descrierea CIP a Bibliotecii Naţionale a României
LILIAN DAYTON
   PUBLISHING IMPRINT. The Ultimate Guide on How to Publish Faster to Make More Profit, Learn Effective Strategies on How to Come up and Publish Content Faster. / Lilian Dayton –
Bucharest: Editura My Ebook, 2021
   ISBN

LILIAN DAYTON

PUBLISHING IMPRINT

The Ultimate Guide on How to Publish Faster to Make More Profit, Learn Effective Strategies on How to Come up and Publish Content Faster

My Ebook Publishing House
Bucharest, 2021

CONTENTS

CONTENTS

INTRODUCTION

As one of the most important elements of online marketing success, content can consume vast amounts of time and energy. It's not unusual for a business owner to spend several hours a day brainstorming, writing, and publishing their content.

While you can't really eliminate your need for content, you can reduce the amount of time you spend on it. By embracing tips, tactics, and systems that support you and your business, it's safe to say that you can cut your content time in half and still create the same great content you've been creating.

Your time is precious. By becoming more efficient and productive, you're able to reallocate that time you saved on content to other profitable tasks. For example, if you're a coach and you free up 5 hours a week, you can spend those five hours coaching clients and making money.

Of course, if you're looking for a way to enjoy a shorter work week, you can use those five hours spending time with friends, family and enjoying personal pursuits. So, let's get to it. The Speedy Content Publishing Tips are divided into the following sections:

- *Brainstorming* – learn to brainstorm faster and more efficiently.

- *Writing* – Yes, you can write more quickly and still create exceptional content.

- *Researching* – Too many people waste precious time researching. Learn how to find what you need quickly and painlessly.

- *Organizing* – Proven tips to organize your content for productivity and efficiency.

- *Publishing* – You can even save time when you publish your content.

Let's dive right in and start with what can be the most difficult part of the content process, brainstorming.

CHAPTER 1

Time Saving Tips, Ideas, and Tactics
to Brainstorm Your Content

Do you have a regular content brainstorming session or do you simply let the ideas come to you? There's no "right" way to brainstorm content. However, there are steps that you can take to make the process more efficient and also more effective.

#1 Be Prepared

Many busy entrepreneurs find that the best content ideas come to them when they're not working. Maybe you're at a family picnic or sitting in traffic. You're thinking about your business and a brilliant idea comes to you.

If you're not prepared to document the idea, chances are you'll forget it by the time you get home. And let's face it, it's easy to believe you'll remember the idea – after all, it's a great one. However, most often the idea fades away.

One of the fastest ways to brainstorm content is to keep a running list of ideas. The ideas may not be complete thoughts, but the concept can help you brainstorm content when it's time to sit down and get to work.

So how do you prepare to capture every content idea when it comes to you?

- *Notebook* – yep, good old fashioned pen and paper still work
- *Phone* – even a simple note-taking application can be useful
- *Voice mail* - leave yourself a voice mail if you don't have an opportunity to write down your idea
- *Email* – send yourself an email. That way, it's waiting for you when you get back to your home office.

#2 Monthly or Weekly Ideas Session

Do you find that there is a particular day of the week or the month where you're usually motivated and inspired? For example, after the weekend, many entrepreneurs are ready to get back to work. Monday and Tuesday are often exciting and motivating days. By the end of the week things can wind down.

Identify your best time to brainstorm and capitalize on your energy by scheduling a brainstorming session.

When brainstorming:

- **Set Aside A Moderate Amount Of Time**. An hour or two is probably long enough to brainstorm. Your mind will start to wander and you'll stop being productive. Don't worry, once you've started the creative process, more ideas will come to you throughout your day.

- **Go To An Inspiring Location To Brainstorm**. Imagine trying to brainstorm content ideas as children are running circles around you as you sit at the kitchen table. Not very productive. Instead, find a peaceful place where you feel inspired. Put on some music if it's not distracting; kick your feet back and begin thinking about the various types of content you can create to help your audience.

- **Review Analytics.** Great ideas are often inspired by past successes. Look at the content that received the best comments, links, and feedback. Review your analytics to find your most popular articles or posts and brainstorm more ideas on the topics.

- **Use Creativity Tools.** There are many different brainstorming tools to consider. For example, mind mapping is quite popular. You can also use a vision board or even creative prompts. You can create your own brainstorming tools, too. For example, you might create a series of flash cards that ask questions like: What problem is my ideal customer facing today?

- **Identify Inspiration**. Are there certain blogs, magazines, or websites that frequently inspire you? If so, organize them into a folder on your search engine toolbar. Create a folder to make them easy to access. And yes, your competition may be a key source of content inspiration.

#3 Broaden Your Horizons

One of the reasons it can become tricky to brainstorm ideas is because people get stuck in a rut. They create the same type of content over and over again. Remember you can create:

- Audio
- Video
- Lists
- Tips

- Content series
- Worksheets
- Editorials
- Q&A
- Interviews
- Info graphics
- How To articles
- Reviews

And much more. As you're struggling to come up with ideas, try to create ideas for many different formats. You may find that a "tips" article fits nicely with an interview and create a sense of cohesion and flow on your blog or website.

Brainstorming can often be a frustrating process. Embrace systems and tools that support you to succeed. Additionally, if you find you're having a tough time coming up with ideas, take a break or consider outsourcing the topic idea research for a month or two. You may simply need to step back and look at your audience and niche from a fresh perspective.

So once you have your list of content ideas and topics, it's time to sit down and start creating the content. Let's take a look at a few proven methods for enjoying productive writing sessions.

CHAPTER 2

How to Write Quickly - Get Your Thoughts and Ideas onto the Page and Published In Less Time

How long does it take you to write a blog post or article? For many business owners, the answer is an hour or more. Yet an experienced writer can write three quality blog posts in the same amount of time. It's not because they're better writers. Rather, it's because they have embraced writing systems and practices that support productivity.

As you read through the following ideas, know that not all of them will work for you. However, if you're able to embrace just a few of them, you'll cut your writing time down significantly.

#1 Work in Batches

Joe is a business owner and writes all his own content. On a productive day, Joe can write four or five blog posts in an hour. The trick that works for him is to focus on writing his content in batches.

For example, he might spend an hour writing reviews. Later, when he sits back down to his writing desk he might focus on writing a handful of tips articles.

There are many reasons why this system works. One of the primary reasons is that the batch approach doesn't require Joe to shift focus. In his case, each article in a batch has the same basic format. He can approach them almost as if he's writing from a template.

Batching content by format isn't the only approach you can take. You can batch by topic or subject matter as well. For example, someone in a coaching niche might focus on writing motivation content for the first hour. When they return to their computer they might shift gears and focus on writing a few how to stay confident articles.

#2 Set a Time Limit and Goal

Another common practice is to set a time limit for your writing session. Give yourself an hour to write and set a goal. For example, if you're writing a report, then maybe you want to have three pages completed by the end of your hour.

Once the hour is up, get up and take a break. Nothing slows down the writing process faster than forcing yourself to sit at your desk and write until you're bleary eyed and exhausted.

If an hour seems like too long, set a timer for twenty or thirty minutes. Experiment and find a length and goal that works for you.

#3 Outline First

You can make writing a speedier process by outlining the content first. You don't have to get too detailed with your outline, unless you want to. What's most important is to identify the key points you want to make in your piece.

That generally includes your subtitles and bullet points.

An outline helps you stay focused on what you want to say. You may likely find that you don't pause to determine what you want to say next because it's already outlined. You can flow from one point to the next without stopping.

#4 Templates

If you tend to write similarly formatted content, consider creating templates. For example, a review article or blog post will likely have a recognizable structure. You can visit the reviews you've already written and published and use them to create a template for future reviews.

The same is true for how to articles, tips articles, and lists and so on. A template approach means you simply have to fill in the blanks and can really speed up the writing process.

#5 Eliminate Distractions

It's tempting to sit down in front of the television at night and work on tomorrow's blog post. However, it'll take you five times longer to write that blog post than if you wrote it without distractions.

You see, contrary to what many people have been taught, multitasking really isn't possible. Each time you pull your eyes away from the television to write, you have to shift focus. It may take an entire hour to write an article if you're distracted. Sit down in a quiet place and it may take you a mere ten to fifteen minutes.

Distractions aren't always on television. Consider the following and ask yourself if they're distractions for you:

- Email
- Social media
- Music
- Phone
- Family members
- Chores

You may find that the longer you sit at the desk trying to write, the easier it is to be distracted. The next tip may be a perfect solution for you.

#6 Write When You Can Focus

Are you a night owl? A morning person? Chances are there is a time of day that you feel more focused and productive. And there's a time of day when all you want to do is take a nap.

The ideal time to write is when you feel focused. That might be first thing in the morning if that's when you're most alert. Get to know your personal productivity patterns and schedule writing time when you're more likely to be successful.

#7 Be Opportunistic

Are you having a creative day? Are you feeling inspired or motivated to write? Seize those moments and capitalize on them. Those are the days when content will flow freely and you'll be able to write quickly.

Even if you don't "need" to write, allow yourself the opportunity to get ahead on your content. Or create something extra. Additionally, if you find you have free time during your week, and you're feeling productive, use it to create content. Be opportunistic.

#8 Write Now, Edit Later

Do you find yourself rewriting the same sentence several times because you're trying to make it grammatically correct? Do you use spellcheck more often than the "enter" key on your keyboard? If this sounds like you then you may benefit from trying this tactic.

Write your entire piece of content without editing anything. Let all those red lines under misspelled words sit there without being corrected. Don't run to your thesaurus or your Chicago Manual of Style. Just write.

Once the content is completed, then go ahead and start the editing process. Use your spellcheck. Fix awkward sentences and format the content the way you want to.

The reason this approach works is simple.

Each time you halt the writing process and edit, you're stopping the thought flow. When it's time to return to the writing process and putting words on paper, you have to shift gears again. It may not seem like the shift in focus is significant, however it does slow you down.

Give it a try. You may be surprised by how quickly you are able to write content when you don't stop to edit. In fact, you may need to experiment with several of these tactics to find the strategies that work best for you. For example, you may find that outlining your content actually slows down your writing process because you feel too restricted. Conversely, you may also find that working in batches cuts your writing time in half.

Because content often needs to help establish credibility and authority, it's important to take a look at the content research process. This is where many people lose precious time.

CHAPTER 3

Bogged Down By Research?
6 Tips to Make the Process Fast and Painless

Let's be blunt here for a second. You can waste tons of time researching your content. In fact, it's not uncommon for someone to spend twice as much time researching for their content than writing it. That's precious time. Time you could be spending doing something much more fun and interesting.

#1 Write First, Research Later

One common suggestion is to write your content first. Write what you know and say what you want to say. As you're writing your content, whenever you come to a point where you want to insert a statistic or share data, highlight it. Continue writing.

Once you've finished the piece, then hit the search engines and find those key data points you want to share. This helps you save time because instead of looking for random information, you know exactly what information you need to search for. You'll spend a few minutes researching instead of a few hours.

#2 Find and Bookmark Key Resources

Depending on your niche, there are likely a few reputable resources you can turn to. For example, if you're in the nutrition industry, then you might turn to Harvard's Health Letter for information. If you're in the dog niche, then perhaps you turn to the American Veterinary Association or Cesar Millan. Identify your key sources and bookmark them. This makes it very easy for you to locate information from trusted resources.

#3 Use a Search Friendly Browser

Some web browsing tools are easier to use than others. When you're researching online try a few tools. For example, if you often use Chrome, then try Bing or Firefox. Use a browser that allows you to open multiple tabs. This makes it easy to find, and keep, the information you need.

#4 Note Taking Software and Applications

Do you have a system for organizing your research? Consider using a tool like EverNote, https://evernote.com/ , or Microsoft's One Note, http://office.microsoft.com/en-us/onenote/. These tools make note taking and research easy. You can also use them in combination with your topic brainstorming sessions.

For example, as you're making your list of content topics for the month, you can also identify key sites for information and even outline your content in the note taking application.

Technology can make the content creation process streamlined and efficient.

#5 Source Your Information

Always give credit where credit is due. For example, as you're writing your article on puppy care, if you use data from the American Veterinary Association, then source it and let your readers know where you found your information.

As you're researching for your content, take notes on the relevant and useful information and don't forget to note where you found the information. Then, you can be sure you're linking to the appropriate website or person and it makes it easier to go back to verify the information.

Research doesn't have to take long. In fact, ideally it should only take a minute or two per content piece. Organize your favorite sites, document your sources, and research only the information you know you need to save the most time. Speaking of organization, your systems are an important element of success.

CHAPTER 4

Organization Matters – How to Organize Your Content for Productivity and Efficiency

You may not realize it, but how you organize your content creation process makes a huge difference in your productivity. A simple example of this is the person who sits down in the morning to write the day's blog post. They have no idea what they're going to write about, what the goal is, and where they're going to get their information. The blog post takes much longer than it should to write.

Conversely, the business owner who has an editorial calendar that includes the topic idea, a brief outline, monetization strategy, goals, and a publication date will likely be much more productive. Organize your systems well enough and you can still procrastinate on your content, write it the day it's due, and still only spend a few minutes on the task.

#1 Editorial Calendar

A simple editorial calendar is a list of the dates you want to publish each piece of content. You can create an editorial calendar for the week, month, quarter, or even an annual calendar. You can create it on a simple calendar tool like Microsoft Outlook or Excel or you can use project management software like Basecamp to establish deadlines. And if you enjoy pen and paper, then grab a printable calendar.

You can take the basic editorial calendar and make it more useful by adding the following information.

- Article Topic
- Key Points/Outline
- Data/Information Resources
- Monetization strategy
- Goals for content
- Call to action
- Embedded links
- Template/format

The more you can predetermine about your content, the easier it will be to write it. When you have the topic, structure, research and goals identified, it can literally take you just a few minutes to create your content.

Let's talk a minute about monetization. Each piece of content that you publish whether it's PLR, Video, or content you've written should have a goal. What do you want it to achieve? What do you want readers to do?

In many cases, you simply want people to read the content and click on a link to make a purchase or earn you a commission. You want to monetize the content. There are many different ways to monetize your content. Plan ahead and you can craft your content to fit your chosen monetization tactic.

- Ad Placement – You can use various plugins or widgets to integrate advertisements right into the body of your content. For example, EmbedAds, http://wordpress.org/plugins/embad/, is a WordPress plugin that gives you control over where and when your ads are displayed.

- Promotional Offers – Does your content lead into a click to a sales page or a promotional offer? You can include that offer right in the closing of your content or create your own promotional advertisements or messages and embed them with a widget or plugin.

- Subscription – Do you have a membership site? If so, you can motivate subscriptions by providing a teaser or a portion of an article and making the rest of the content available with a paid subscription.

- AdSense – Google's advertising plan for publishers, https://www.google.com/adsense/, is still alive and strong as a monetization model for many online businesses.

- WordPress Plugins – There are also plugins you can install on your WordPress site that identify keywords and attach relevant links to those keywords. Skimlinks, http://wordpress.org/plugins/skimlinks/, and Amazon Auto Links are two examples of this type of monetization plugin.

Not all content needs to be monetized. However, it is an important consideration when you're planning your content, choosing your topics, and establishing goals.

#2 Note Taking Systems

Tools like Evernote and OneNote have already been discussed. These tools allow you to

- Save your ideas – for example a brilliant content idea that came to you during your morning walk

- They can be accessed anywhere – Evernote and Onenote both have mobile applications that link to your account. No matter what device you're using to take notes and capture ideas, you can access them from one single account.

- Search by Keyword – Note taking tools make it easy to find things fast. You can search by keyword, tag or even printed and handwritten text inside images. No more shuffling through papers on your desk to find your lists and ideas.

Note taking applications aren't for everyone. If you find yourself using pen and paper more often than a device, that's fine. The important step here is to create a system that works for you.

Some people find a three ring binder is the perfect system to take and organize their notes.

#3 Project Management

If you utilize contractors, for example ghostwriters, editors, graphic designers or virtual assistants, then a project management system will be valuable for you on many levels. There are both free and paid Project management tools.

For example, Google Drive can be used as a project management tool. It has a calendar and document system that you can share with specific people – even if they don't have a google account or Gmail address.

There are also WordPress plugins for project management. For example, WP Project Manager, http://wordpress.org/plugins/wedevs-project-manager/, lets you assign projects, create lists and milestones and upload files.

Basecamp is an online project management and collaboration tool, http://basecamp.com/. If you're looking for a tool to help combine communication and project management with your contractors and you want to organize your content, a project management software or service can be a big help. You can use the milestone feature to schedule content creation and publication. You can upload relevant documents, for example, your outline and monetization tactic, for each piece of content. And you can use the system to document your results as well.

Create an organization system that supports your personal work style. You may enjoy organizing everything digitally or you may have a file cabinet that Martha Stewart would be proud of. A system must support you to follow through and actually use it. And that brings us to the last step in the content process – publishing.

CHAPTER 5

Publishing Your Content – The Last Step, Almost

Once you've gone through the work of creating your content, the next step is to make it available to your audience. It's time to publish. In general, the publication process doesn't take too long. However, there are a few time-saving tips you can embrace here as well. Heck, every minute you save is a minute you can spend doing something else for your business or for yourself.

#1 Use a Plugin

There are WordPress Plugins that take the work out of uploading and publishing content. Some work like a content management system and create custom field types. Your content is automatically optimized and organized on your site by type. Ultimate CMS, http://wordpress.org/plugins/ultimate-cms/ is one example of a content management plugin as is My Content Management, http://wordpress.org/plugins/my-content-management/.

SEO plugins help you optimize the content for search engines. All in One SEO, http://wordpress.org/plugins/all-in-one-seo-pack/ is a popular WordPress plugin.

Additionally, there are plugins like APLC Speedy Publisher, http://contentrix.com/aplc-speedy- publisher/254 that make it possible to upload several articles or posts at once.

Plugins can make the data entry aspect of content publishing much more efficient.

#2 Pre-Schedule

WordPress allows website owners to pre-schedule their content. This means you can upload a month's worth of content in one sitting and be done with it. Of course, this means that you need to have a content plan and have written your content in advance. It may take a little time to adopt this type of content writing and publishing system. However, once you make it part of your routine you'll realize how much time you can save. The next challenge will be to decide what you're going to do with all that free time.

#3 Outsource It

Once the content is created, you can outsource the publishing to someone else. In fact, if you have a skilled virtual assistant, you might hire them to edit, format, and publish your content. This gives you the free time you need to brainstorm, plan, create and enjoy the profits.

Ideally, publishing your content will be the step you spend the least amount of time on. Explore the technology available to reduce your time and effort.

So, What's The Last Step?

The last step of the content process is to test and track your results. Not only do you want to create systems and use analytics to track the success of each piece of content, you also want to test and track your content process.

Track the time it takes you to brainstorm, write, research, and publish. Look for ways you can optimize your new systems to save even more time. Remember, each hour you cut can be an hour spent making money or pursuing other interests.

Content is so important to a business, but publishing it shouldn't be a chore. With a little planning and using techniques and tools that support you and your business you can make quick work of writing and publishing your content.

BONUS CHAPTER

Top 10 Digital Publishing Tips

Turning an idea for a book in your head into a successful digital publication requires co- ordinating a whole lot of different steps to create that one hit. Tens of thousands of digital books are published *every month*, but only a fraction of them will sell more than a thousand copies.

How do you make sure your book is one of the few that succeeds? How do you hit the top charts? How do you sell and sell and sell your books, even if you don't have a brand or a reputation to rely on now?

These ten digital publishing tips will help you do just that.

Tip #1: Everything You Need to Know About Pricing

How you price your book makes a big impact on your sales and your ultimate profits. Here's what you need to know about pricing.

Most first-time authors should price their books at around the $2.99 price range. Go a little higher if you're in a high end market or if your book is especially thick.

On the other hand, if you're a well known author or if you're publishing highly specialized knowledge for which there are no other alternative titles, then price your book more towards the $9.99 range.

If you're looking to use your book to get as many readers as possible without much care for how much profit you actually make, then by all means go ahead and publish it for $0.99 cents or for free.

Tip #2: More on $0.99 Cent Books

It's very difficult to make a profit on $0.99 cent books. The commissions you'll have to pay to the bookstores will cut your profits down even further until the amount you make per sale is completely negligible.

For example, on the Amazon Kindle store when you price your books at $0.99 you'll only get paid a 35% royalty. That means that when all is said and done, you'll only be making around 30 cents per download.

If you plan on making a living selling books, this price point just doesn't work.

However, the one notable exception is if you want to use this price to get more people into your sales funnel or brand umbrella. For example, you might sell your primary book for $8.99, then publish 5 much smaller books on specific topics all priced at $0.99. People who buy your cheaper book who want to learn more can do so by purchasing your more expensive book.

Use the $0.99 price point as a marketing tool, rather than as a profit strategy.

Tip #3: Hire a Professional Proofreader

Proofreading your own books is not a good idea. Neither is sending it to your friend to see if they spot any mistakes. A professional proofreader can turn a good piece of content into something truly phenomenal. If you're serious about your book's success, hire a great proofreader to look your work over.

There are a few different ways to find proofreaders.

For one, you can use a service like Proofreading Pal (http://www.proofreadingpal.com) to do it.

These kinds of companies hire dozens of proofreaders and make them available for projects for a small markup.

Alternatively, you can head over to a freelancer marketplace like eLance (http://www.elance.com) and find a proofreader to hire. Make sure you look through their before and after samples before making a decision.

Tip #4: Read it on the Digital Device

If you're publishing your book on the Kindle, read it on the Kindle. If you're publishing it on the Nook, read it on the Nook. The same goes for an iBookstore book.

Just because your book looks great on screen doesn't mean it'll look good on a digital device. Make sure you read your book the way your audience will be reading it.

Both Barnes & Nobles and Amazon have basic devices you can purchase for under $150. If you don't care to own the devices, you can just buy the device and sell it on Craigslist or eBay immediately after testing your books. The difference between purchase price and sale price usually won't be more than $40.

Tip #5: Plant a Teaser for Your Site

Put a teaser for your site in your book. For example, let's say you're publishing a book about fishing. Your book goes in depth into details on everything from rod selection to actual fishing techniques.

However, there are a few things you don't cover. You don't cover how to choose a fishing boat. You don't cover how to predict the best weather for fishing.

Instead of putting these things in your book, you tell them you've put them in a separate report that's available for free on your website. People who read your book will then go to your website to get those freebies.

You can require people to give you their email address before they receive the freebies. Because they've already paid for your content and already have a level of trust built in for you, your opt-in rate will be very high.

Tip #6: Make Your Samples Pack a Punch

It's not uncommon in physical books for people to spend the first few pages ramping up. You might talk about fundamental concepts or use the first few pages to get your readers in the right mindset to learn.

With digital books however, this is a bad strategy. Your first few pages are going to be your preview pages, which means

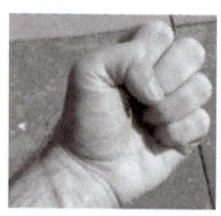

that for first few pages have to *pack an emotional punch*. People who read just your first few pages should feel inspired or excited. They should want to get the rest of your book.

Don't write your first 5 pages for people who've already purchased your book. Instead, write them for people who're considering buying your book. Consider it a sales-oriented piece of high quality content.

Tip #7: Outsource the Formatting Cheaply

If you're not great at formatting your books, why not just have someone else do it for you?

Head over to Fiverr (http://www.fiverr.com) or eLance (http://www.elance.com) and look for people who offer to format digital book. You can easily find someone who'll format your digital book for under $20. In fact, on Fiverr you'll often be able to format your books for just $5.

They'll insert the page breaks, create the Table of Contents, make sure your chapter headings appear correctly, so on and so forth.

Formatting eBooks is one of the most common obstacles writers face in getting published. There are people who specialize in doing just this. Why not let the specialists handle it (cheaply) so you can focus on writing and marketing?

Tip #8: Target Peripheral Markets

One great way to get more people to read your books is to target peripheral markets.

For example, let's say you have a primary book about weight loss that's selling for $8.99. Instead of just continually publishing books about weight loss, why not target a few peripheral markets?

For example, publish a book about weight loss over 45, publish a book about weight loss for people with diabetes and publish a book about weight loss for mothers who've just had a child.

Each of these books can help build your brand, as well as get more people to purchase your main product.

Tip #9: Participate in Platform Communities

Each platform has a community. For example, there are many places where Kindle authors can go to network with other authors. Be an active member of these communities.

There are a few powerful ways that these communities can help you:

- You can learn a lot from past questions and posts. If you have a question, chances are someone else has already asked that question at some point.

- You can ask questions. If you ever get stuck in the publishing or marketing process, just reach out for help.

- You can ask for feedback. Not sure if your book, your cover or your marketing strategy is up to snuff? You can just ask.

- You can find partnership opportunities. If you and another author are in the same market, why not pool your resources so you both come out ahead?

- You can ask for reviews. Ask other authors to purchase your book and review you, and you'll do the same.

The list of potential benefits goes on and on. Participating in these communities is a key to success on any platform.

Tip #10: Watch Your Reports and Optimize for What's Working

Watch your sales reports carefully. Track all your marketing activities and try to draw links between your sales and what you did to generate those sales.

If you go on several internet podcasts to market your book and see no spike in sales, you probably won't want to spend time doing podcast interviews in the future.

On the other hand, if you write a few guest articles for industry websites and suddenly see a flood of sales, that'd probably be a good avenue to focus on in the future.

Watch for unexpected stats. For example, if you're publishing your book primarily for the US market but suddenly notice an influx of sales from the UK, ask yourself why. Did someone in the UK pick up and promote your book? Did it strike a cord among an unexpected audience?

Try to figure out what's working and do more of that. Also, try to figure out what doesn't work and stop doing it.

If you follow these ten tips, you'll be one of the few self-published authors who knows both how to write a great book and how to run a great book *business*. Follow these tips and you'll create a fantastic product that generates sales, month in and month out.

Printed by Libri Plureos GmbH in Hamburg, Germany